SILLY JOKES FOR 7 YEAR OLDS

Why did the woman bring some tea to the birthday party?

She was a par-tea person!

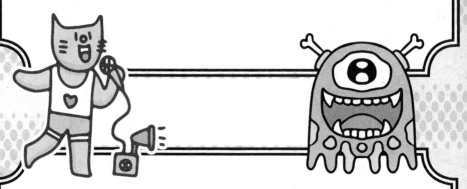

What type of tea do football players love the most?

Penal-tea!

What did the fish in the tank say to the others?

Do any of you know how to drive this thing?!

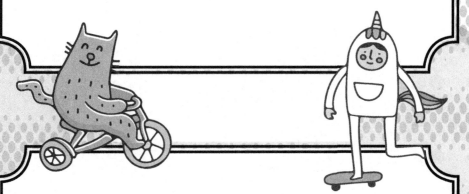

Why did the merchants buy a ship online?

There was a huge sail!

What should you call a rabbit that is a transformer?

Hop-timus Prime!

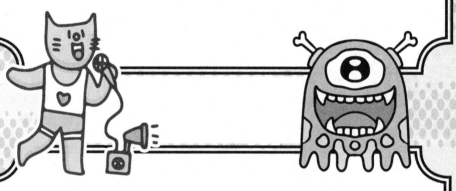

If a boomerang doesn't come back, what should you call it?

A stick!

Where can astronaut cows go to get a drink?

The Milky Way!

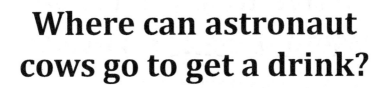

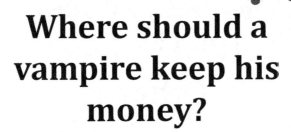

Where should a vampire keep his money?

In the blood bank!

What did the tree say when it went furniture shopping?

Please pass me the cata-log!

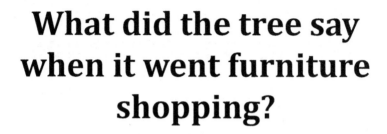

Knock, knock.
Who's there?
Orange.
Orange who?
Orange you going to say hello to me?!

What made the chewing gum cross the road?

It got stuck under the chicken's feet!

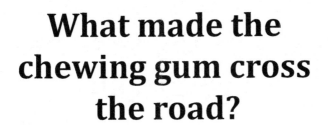

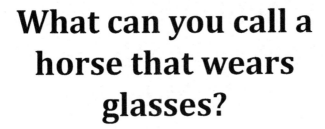

What can you call a horse that wears glasses?

A see-horse!

What was the first animal to go to space?

That cow who jumped over the moon!

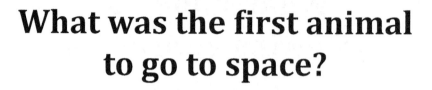

Which side of a turkey has the most feathers?

The outside!

What do traffic police use in the North Pole?

Snow cones!

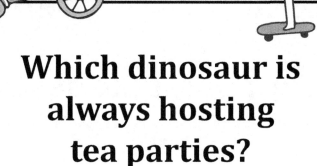

Which dinosaur is always hosting tea parties?

The Tea-Rex!

What happens if you cut your cake with a hammer?

It becomes pound cake!

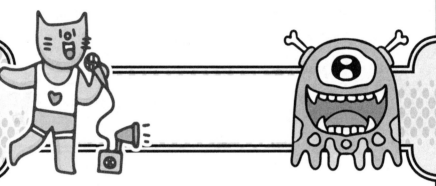

Why is a cat the best at video games?

Because it always gets nine lives!

Which juice do ponies love to drink?

Lemon-neigh'd!

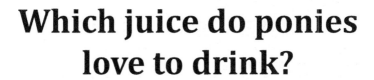

Knock, knock.
Who's there?
Donut.
Donut, who?
Donut even think about opening your presents until Christmas!

What is the best lunch to give to ninjas?

Kung-food!

What can you call a Buffalo that eats lots of beef?

A Beef-alo!

Why are quarters so silly?

They don't have any cents!

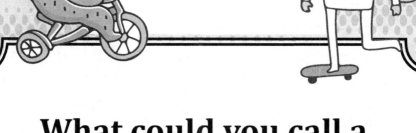

What could you call a cow that can't make milk?

An udder failure!

Which party snack do snow people love?

Ice Krispy Treats!

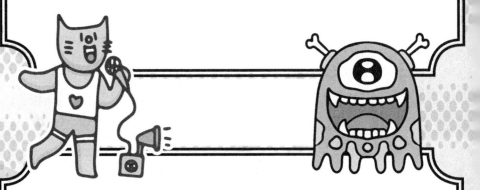

How do you know when a vampire is sick?

Because they're always coffin!

What is colorful and goes round and round?

A toucan stuck in a tumble dryer!

What food tastes the best in winter?

Brrrrrrr-gers!

What do rabbits use instead of combs?

Hare brushes!

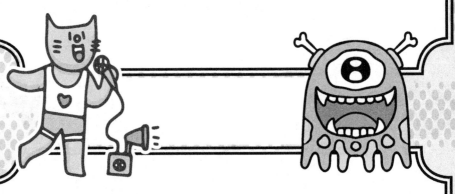

What can you call a monkey that explodes?

A bab-boom!

Guess what my horse's favorite sport is...

Stable tennis!

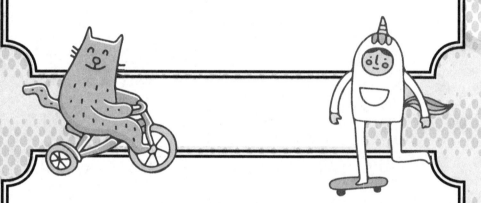

What do mountains wear to keep warm in winter?

Snowcaps!

Why did the dinosaur have to cross the road?

The chicken wasn't even born yet!

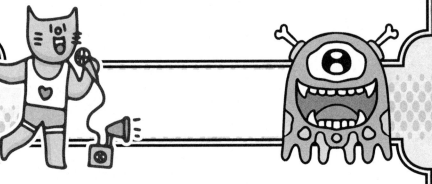

Knock, Knock.
Who's there?
Jester.
Jester who?
Jester moment, I can't find my keys!

Where does a pig eskimo live?

In a pig-loo!

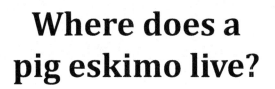
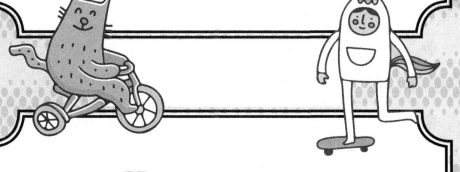

How can you throw a great space party?

Planet very early!

Why were there holes in the book about apples?

Because of all the bookworms!

What did the kitten say when it finished dessert?

That was very mice!

What sport do insects love the most?

Cricket!

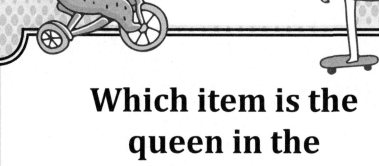

Which item is the queen in the classroom?

The ruler!

What made the lion cross over the road?

It had to get to the other pride!

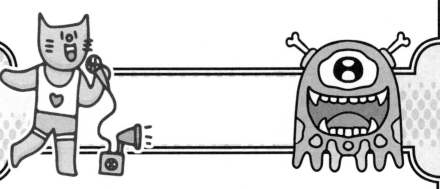

What would a horse say if it fell over?

I have fallen and can't giddy up!

Why should you be very careful on grass?

Because of all the blades!

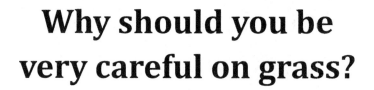

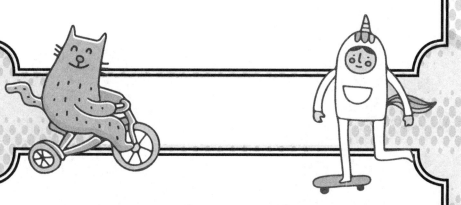

How does a bee get to school?

It takes the school buzz!

Which type of race can't you run in?

A swimming race!

How does a penguin builder make his house strong?

Igloos it!

What is black, white and gets red all over?

A newspaper!

Who brings the elephants all of their Christmas presents?

Elephanta Claus!

What does a football player always wear on halloween?

A face mask!

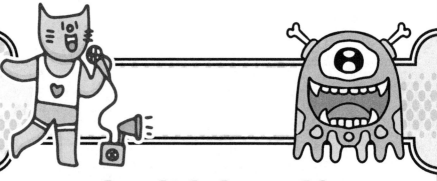

Why did the golfer have to wear two pairs of pants?

In case she got a hole in one!

How can dogs take a break when watching their favorite show?

By pressing the paws button!

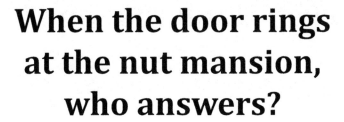

When the door rings at the nut mansion, who answers?

The peanut buttler!

What is the best move for a pig that knows karate?

The pork chop!

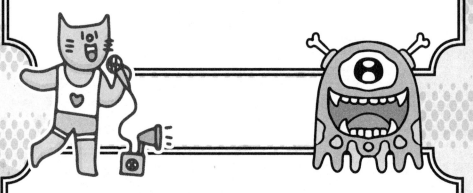

Do you think that one bird can make a pun?

No, but I am sure that toucan!

What would a raincloud wear under their clothes?

Thunderwear!

What goes "woof, wooo, woof, wooo"?

A dog whistle!

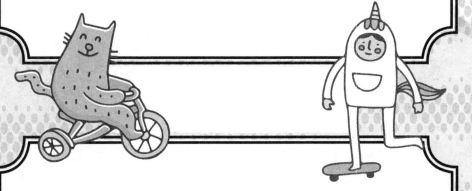

Where should a sheep go to get a haircut?

To the baaa-baaa shop!

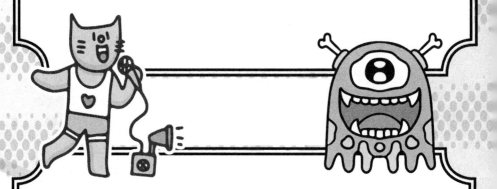

What would you get if you had 50 cookies and you ate 40 of them?

A belly ache!

Why shouldn't you talk to circles?

Because there is never any point!

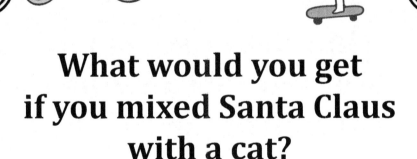

What would you get if you mixed Santa Claus with a cat?

Santa Claws!

How can you get a tissue to start dancing?

Just put a boogie in it!

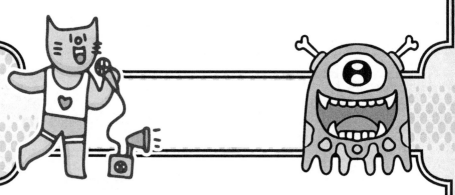

How does the Cookie Monster feel after he's eaten all of the cookies?

Very crummy!

Do you think you'll remember me in a year? Yes.
Do you think you'll remember me in a month? Yes.
Do you think you'll remember me in a week? Yes.
Do you think you'll remember me in a day? Yes.

Knock, knock.
Who's there?
Wow! You already forgot me!

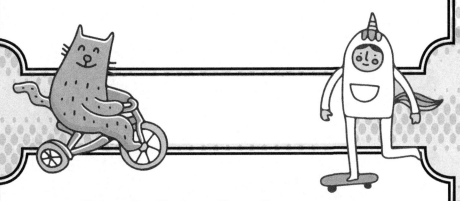

Which kind of sports car do cats love to drive?

Fur-arris!

What kind of candy can arrest you?

A lolli-cop!

What sort of plates do they use to serve cake on Venus?

Flying saucers!

What would go "Ha ha ha..... BANG!"?

A giant laughing their head off!

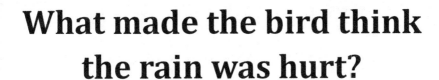

What made the bird think the rain was hurt?

Because it saw the rain fall!

Doctor, doctor, I'm so scared of squirrels!

Doctor: Well, you must be completely nuts!

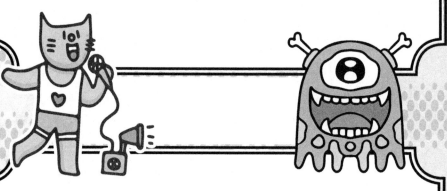

Why did the crab have to go to prison?

Because it kept on pinching things!

What could you call a bunch of monkeys who win the World Cup?

The World Chimp-ions!

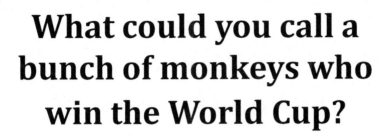

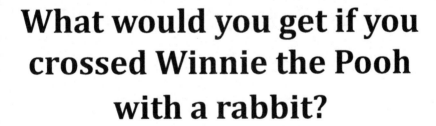

What would you get if you crossed Winnie the Pooh with a rabbit?

A honey bunny!

What should you call a fish that has four eyes?

A fiiiish!

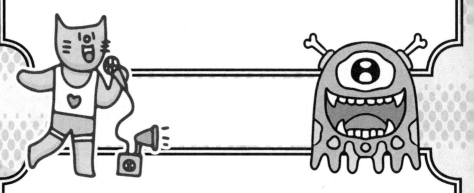

What should you call someone who has a nose but no body?

No-body nose!

Why does a swan have to have so many feathers?

To cover their butt quacks!

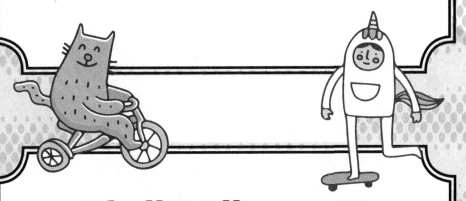

Shall I tell you my favorite pizza joke?

Actually, forget it, it's too cheesy!

Where do the mice that love computers hang out?

On their mouse-pads!

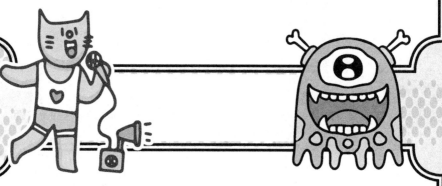

What would you call a dinosaur that always destroys things?

A Tyrannosaurus-Wrecks!

Where can hamburgers go when they feel like dancing?

To the meat-ball!

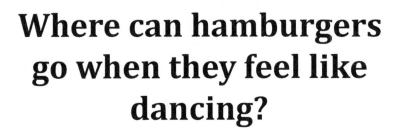

What does Superman eat his cereal from?

A Superbowl!

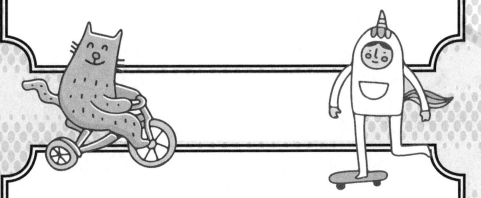

What would a salad say to a tomato after it lost the race?

You really lettuce down!

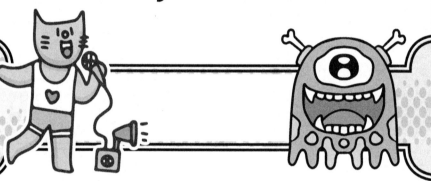

What would the hoop say to a basketball if it missed?

Oh, shoot!

Doctor, Doctor! I feel just like a pair of curtains.

Oh, please! Pull yourself together!

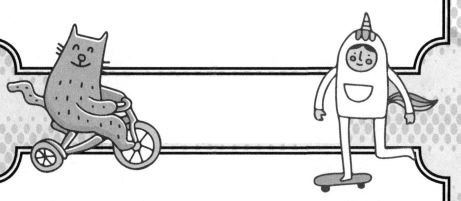

Who cleans the ocean every day?

The mer-maid!

What would a mom bread say to her baby bread?

I loaf you a lot!

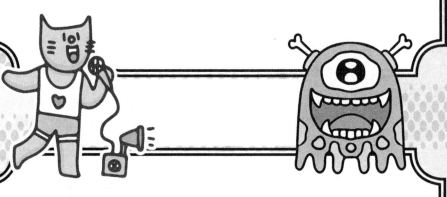

Why didn't the kernel leave the popper?

She became very cornfused!

What could you call a bear with a missing ear?

A B-!

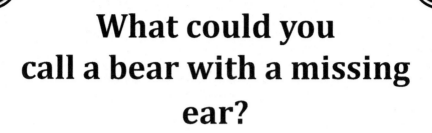

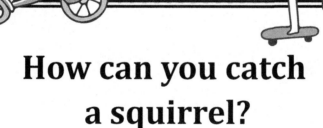

How can you catch a squirrel?

Just climb a tree and act nuts!

What food does a ghost panda eat?

Bam-BOO!

Why wasn't Superman happy with his outfit?

He was too big for the size S!

What would a house always wear for a party?

Ad-dress!

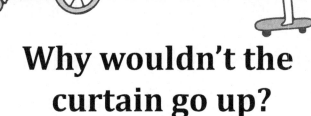

Why wouldn't the curtain go up?

It needed to stretch out!

Why do basketball players make such a mess when they eat?

Because they always dribble!

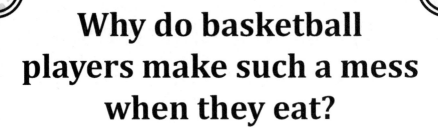

What would you get when you mix Spiderman with corn on the cob?

A cobweb!

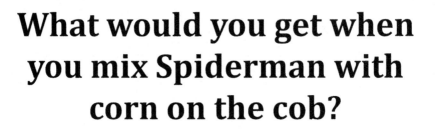

What can you call it when a dinosaur scores a touchdown?

A dino-score!

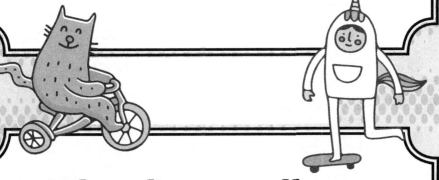

What do you call two birdies who are in love?

Tweethearts!

What would you call a snail that lives at sea?

A snail-or!

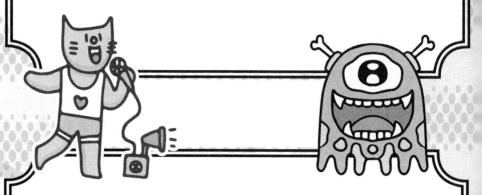

What would you call a dog that can do magic?

A Labracadabra-dor!

Why do witches all wear black dresses at Halloween?

So that no one can tell which witch is which!

Where can you find out where all the apple trees are?

Use a mapple!

How can you fix a pumpkin that is cracked?

Use a pumpkin patch!

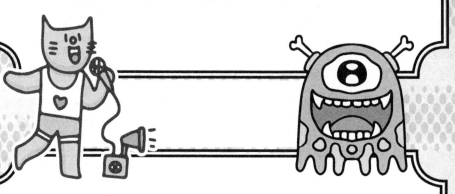

What could you call an elf who is very rich?

Very w-elfy!

What kind of steps should you take when a tiger is running at you?

Big ones!

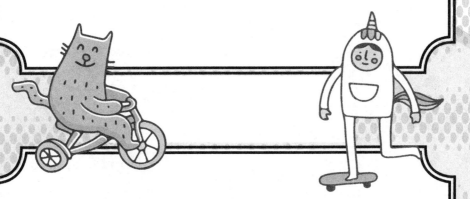

Where do pirates go on holiday?

Arrrrr-gentina!

What do frogs love to eat with their burgers?

French Flies!

What is very heavy and wears glass slippers?

Cinderellephant!

Who won the strongest sea creature contest?

The mussels!

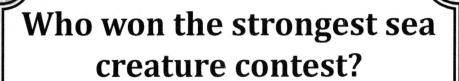

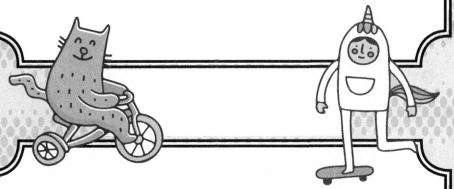

What does a Triceratops usually sit on?

It sits on its Tricera-bottom!

What cookie flavor do monkeys like best?

Chocolate chimp cookies!

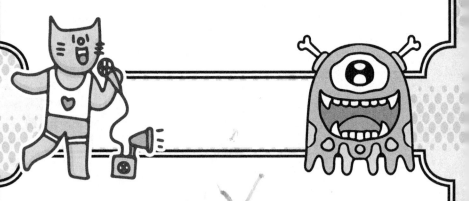

Which day is the best day for visiting the beach?

Sunday!

What type of TVs do ghosts have in their houses?

Big scream TVs!

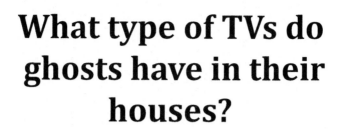

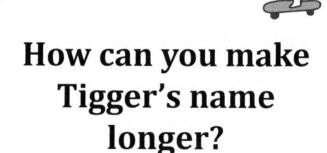

How can you make Tigger's name longer?

Tig-gerrrr!

Which letter is a pirate's favorite?

R!

Which pre-historic creature was the most terrifying?

The Terror-dactyl!

What has hands but cannot clap?

A clock!

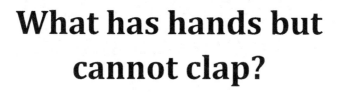

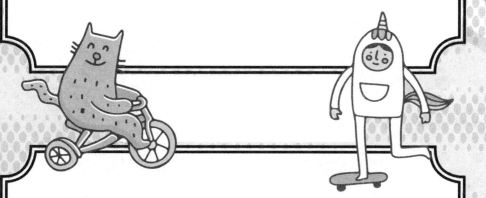

What could you call a sleeping Stegosaurus?

Stego-snorus!

What happens when you wear a sun hat in the rain?

You get a rainbow hat!

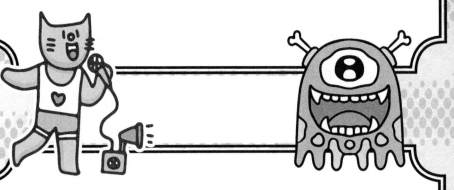

What does a bumble bee say when it scores a touchdown?

Woo! Hive scored!

What did the firefly's friends say about her birthday outfit?

You glow, girl!

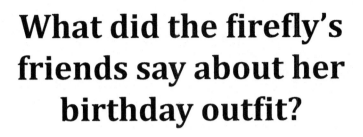

Which kind of sandwich is best for a beach picnic?

Peanut butter & jellyfish!

Which ice cream flavor always gets to the parlor last?

Choco-late!

Why was the bee ready to get married?

Because he found his honey!

Which school contest are skunks the best at?

The smelling bee!

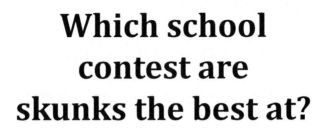

What is a lion with no eyes called?

A Lon!

Which dinosaur are the best police officers?

Tricera-cops

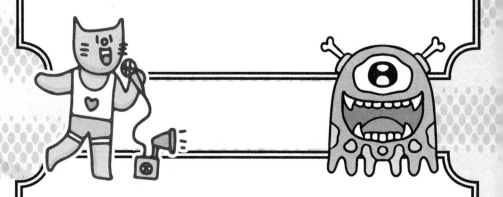

What is a sleeping bull called?

A bull-dozer!

Why do puppies always sit in the front row of class?

Because they love being teacher's pet!

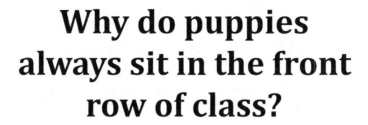

Knock, knock.
Who's there?
Wooden shoe.
Wooden shoe who?
Wooden shoe like to tell me a joke now?

When is seeing a cat bad luck for you?

When you are a mouse!

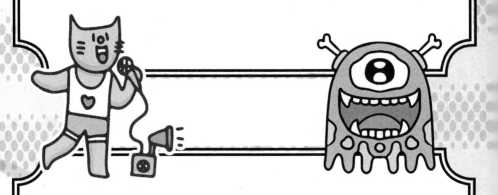

What does a duck use to help with math?

A quack-ulator!

On which day do most people cook fish?

On fry-day!

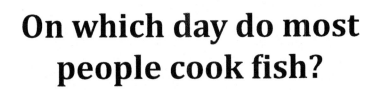

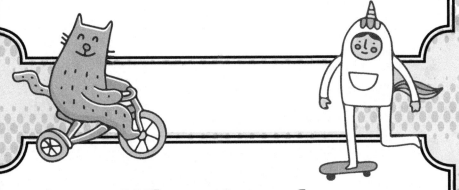

What time do ducks wake up?

Right at the quack of dawn!

What would an owl say to his sweetheart?

You look so hootiful!

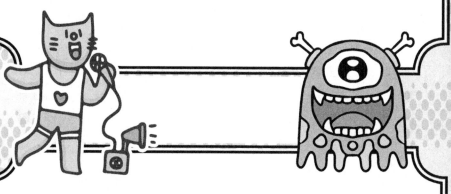

Where would a crew of mice sailors leave their boat?

At the Hickory Dickory Dock!

Why does a dragon have to sleep in the day?

Because they always fight knights!

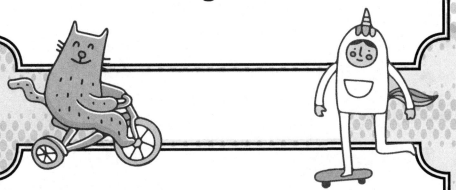

Why does Darth Vader only go out at night?

He always prefers the dark side!

Where does a dinosaur shop for their favorite toys?

Toy-saurus! (Toys 'R' Us)

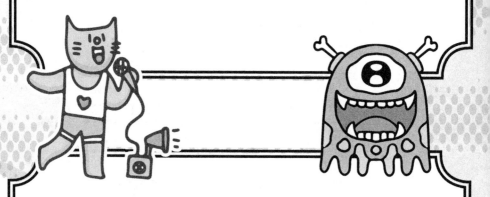

What do you call a turtle who everybody sees on TV?

A shell-ebrity!

Which drink do cows love the best?

A s-moooooo-thie!

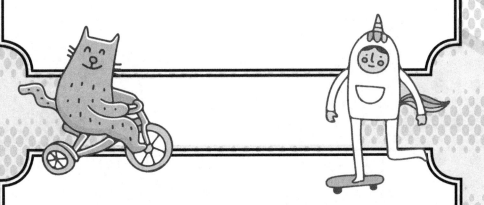

Which bone makes dogs laugh the most?

A funny bone!

Whu did the football quit the team?

You would too if you kept getting kicked around!

Why did the woman say when she threw the clock out of window?

Time has flown by so quickly!

Knock, knock.
Who's there?
Water.
Water who?
Water you doing in there?
Come outside and play!

Why does a toilet
paper always roll
downhill?

It has to get to the bottom!

Which season of the year is the cutest?

Awww-tumn!

Why couldn't the teddy bear eat dessert?

He was already too stuffed!

Where does Spider Man do his online shopping?

On the World Wide Web!

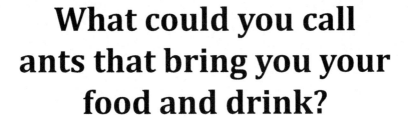

What could you call ants that bring you your food and drink?

Serv-ants!

Printed in Great Britain
by Amazon

37119902R00046